definitions

definitions

Kal Szarkowicz

pet project publishing
Minneapolis, Minnesota

The text of this book was set in Adobe Garamond.

Pet Project Publishing
P.O. Box 19291
Minneapolis, Minnesota 55419

www.petprojectpublishing.com
Printed in the United States of America

16 17 18 19 20 5 4 3 2 1

ISBN: 978-0-692-80694-4
Library of Congress Control Number: 2016959786

this book is dedicated to my family,

who have supported me unconditionally and helped
make this happen for me;

all of my wonderful teachers who have had faith in me
and helped me grow as a person and as a writer;

and to the person who is always my best memory,
even in the worst of times.

Contents

Introduction

Why I Write

I was recently at a writing conference with many well-known authors in the Minnesota area and fellow young writers who someday strive to be sitting in the place of those well-known authors. We are already beginning to find our passions, to discover our voices. It strikes us as welcoming, at first, then overwhelming, but when we learn how far we can take our creativity, it calms us. At least, that is how it works for me.

Here's the thing about being surrounded by thousands of other writers: everyone's different. And if you've ever been a writer, or an artist, or a photographer, or anything remotely creative, I am sure you will agree with me when I say that where there is diversity, there is inspiration. The habits of people never cease to fascinate me, and it is the unknowing, ever-changing world in all its sheer beauty that give me the ideas I use to shape my life into poetry and essays and stories. I will never stop observing where the bus stops on Chicago Avenue at four o'clock in the afternoon, or how the girl who has a new colored scrunchie in her hair every day greets her friends. I will always notice the man walking his pug along our neighborhood sidewalk. I will always find interesting the lives of countless people, performing daily activities, clueless as to how utterly fascinating they are to the wondering eyes of admirers.

I even admire the admirers, in all of their admiring qualities, sitting back and watching those who intrigue them. They strive, they yearn, they observe. They are still someone important, even though they watch someone else. I wish I had a camera in my mind to take snapshots of those people in their own intellectual, spiritual ways, watching themselves do something else besides ache for the place of another. I cherish everyone, in all their own states of being.

It is interesting, seeing how different life is from a bigger picture. Everyone knows that when you look at the big picture, you see how small your conflicts are, especially compared with the problems facing the rest of the world. You see mountains made out of molehills, and if you zoom out far enough, you just might actually find the real mountains that aren't molehills. But those mountains don't belong to you.

The thing some people might not know about the big picture is that as you zoom out of your own snapshot of the world, things sort of disappear. They move very fast before your eyes, and before you know it your landmarks of life are tiny dots. After a while, they just fade away, like the labels of a suburb outside a major city when you zoom out of a map. Once in a while you can zoom back in again, locate the places you left behind, but it's always different. A building or two might've been torn down, or a new school might've been built. The city might've fixed the water pipes on your old street, finally. There are endless possibilities. The point is, when you zoom back in and find that change, your landmarks of life will seem so infinitesimal compared with the world you've seen from its west to its east to its north to its south, wonderfully suffering in all of its beauty and all of its disaster. When you come back to somewhere you left behind, a snapshot frozen in time, you rarely ever want to stay.

I write because I am inspired, solely, by the world. I cannot explain to you exactly what strikes me, but I can tell you it has something to do with mystery, because where there is mystery, there is creative opportunity. Watching the world from the eyes of an admirer is just like seeing a story unfold before your eyes—the story of you, the story of that person over there, the story of the world, the story of another character you've never even heard of but that you are compelled to create—all because of one night of people-watching.

I'm not saying that this has to be everyone's reason for writing. I'm not even saying people have to have a reason; there are parts of my writing that have no reason at all. I am just saying that the totality of the world, in all of its bigness and smallness, in all its wonder and sorrow, is one of the most inspiring things we could ever encounter—and life, the most beautiful thing we reach for when we're pretending it isn't completely intangible.

here lies doubt

nostalgia digs
a shallow grave
for loneliness

it deludes us
into thinking
what we mourn is still here to weep for

but happiness
pats the ground
dry

happiness
comes back every sunday
to deliver flowers

happiness
has healed enough
to smile in spite of itself

happiness
is wise enough
to convince us—

that when we think
we've lost ourselves,
when we think

we are worthless
hopeless
beyond repair;

maybe we aren't looking
hard enough
or maybe

happiness is a house
in a clearing
that we've found without a map

and we're standing on the doorstep, thinking
the lock is broken
but we just lost the right key

that's all.

truth behind terror

fear is our biggest enemy.
it is the weapon we face
and the threat they hold.
their harsh words and violence
fill our eyes that brim with tears.
we breathe their wrath.
our lungs are filled with the smoky
remnants of their ignorance;
and our raw hearts tremble
like puppets they want to play with
to take advantage of our innocence.
they don't know love;
they only know the madness
of wanting power over everything within reach
because deep down
they are helpless.

how to be kind

kindness
is not just about giving
it isn't about sacrifice
it isn't about taking
or owing or returning

kindness
is simply about recognizing
our own lonely hearts
and seeing the resemblance
in another's

it's about someone whose soul
understands you without the words to say so
and embracing it all

moments in oblivion

once upon a time i was innocence—
i was muddy shoes and sandy feet and smiles and laughter;
i was skinned knees and temporary tears
and a pink bicycle with training wheels
that only knew the way up the block and back.

i was the scared pair of eyes that never blinked
in darkness and the fear that held my father's hand at night
while he sang along to my lullabies.
i was happiness, touching the surface of life;
but years passed and i started to recognize
more than just watching the sky for bats at dusk
and being carried out of the car when i fell asleep
and i woke up alone.

life became a reality,
a step out of the world where cicadas buzzed in the sunshine
and breezes drew me into their open arms
like branches of a tree in an offering embrace.
fate became suns that never rose
from the horizon and clouds that moved too slow to vanish
until the sky was a pale white
and the stars fell behind a blanket of tastelessness.

i was a chill even winter had forgotten;
a dream without direction, lost
in the dead of night as it lay
cloaked in the fog of reminiscence.

i was leaves that held onto autumn
before they finally fell at time's feet;
upon a pile of other dormant hearts that had strayed to the
  frozen ground,
one by one
by one.
i was a hope that stood atop a house of glass cards;
my only spectator a pair of empty eyes
whose stare tore deep enough
to tumble the fragile masterpiece to the floor of lies
and raw heartache.

my scars are deeper now
than scratches i used to get when i tripped at the playground,
barely breaking my skin, on the surface of what i once
  thought pain felt like;
now i cry when i hear sad songs on the radio and i spend
  some nights
thinking too much—and
this time, a bandage can't heal my wounds. nothing
  temporary can fix me.

but sometimes in the depths of my longing,
i can still remember what effortless felt like.

it smelled like bug spray
that never seemed to keep the mosquitoes away
and fourth-of-july fireworks that didn't spark high enough
but still left a mark on the driveway when they died.
it was countless coins i threw into fountains,
hoping someday my dreams would come true, but now
i'd give anything just to go back to how it was—
smiling without the flash of a camera
and laughing without the coax of falsity;
when suffering was a faraway sound in my utopia
of wide-eyed wonders and plastic swimming pools and
honeysuckle.

happiness comes in small doses now, coated
with a dust of deceit that time breathes.
i miss the feeling of a warm bath after a long day
and driving around the lake twice
just to catch the last moment of the sunset.

once upon a time,
i was innocence.

expectations

we all paint a picture
of what we visualize our life to be—
but it takes a lifetime to realize
that we don't need all the colors to complete it

broken voices

you were too busy
listening
to your heartbeat
to hear mine
slow down

healing

i was used to grieving with the melancholy songs of the birds
  and then one day i woke up to a silent sky, wondering
why aren't the mourning doves singing anymore?

brooklyn

the city never sleeps, but it dreams
too needed to rest, it grieves
and from its place
it never so much as moves but it changes
it will never win a bet
but it wages

unsent letter

you:

the worst nightmare i've ever dreamt. *(but then i remember that i was awake.)* of course, i never would've guessed you were anything but heavenly. *(and yet, you were an earthquake.)*

you hated how i pined for you. *(but in my defense, you were an ocean and i was a storm.)* you were endless, infinite, and you let me think it's what i needed. *(but in my defense, i just wanted to know what beautiful felt like, even if in the end my small island ended up, by your standards, deformed.)*

you finally cut the rope i was holding onto for so long. *(but in your defense, it was cutting off your circulation.)* you decided, once and for all, that my words didn't fit you anymore. *(though, admittedly, you no longer wanted to be someone's destination.)*

me:

i had begun with a fairy tale and ended in disaster. *(you never wanted anything so destructive.)* i really never bothered to imagine how wonderfully imperfect we were. *(i just thought we could fix the errors if we needed to be constructive.)*

i hated how you rolled your eyes when i tried to challenge you. *(all i wanted was to know you better.)* i wanted a forever, so desperately, and i thought i saw it in you—so you got frightened and lied your way out. *(though you swore you'd never.)*

i finally accepted the way you drank your coffee cold. *(even though you always told me to make it hot.)* i decided, once and for all, that maybe my happy ending wasn't the same as yours. *(it was not.)*

us:

the perfect ending. *(in so many words.)*
you fell and i fell without you.
with every millisecond we faded further and further out
  of sight.
we still fell into the same body of water below.
(but we each swam to a different shore.)

reincarnation

she told me that
in her past life
she was a butterfly

because she remembered
the weightlessness her wings felt
against the summer breeze.

she told me, before she was a butterfly
she was an ocean; and she knew
because she recognized the blue depths and the sloshing of the waves before anyone could even see the storm clouds.

she said that before she was an ocean
she was words;
because she felt them so brilliantly in her veins when she read them, and she spoke them so profoundly

she said that before she was words
she was a blizzard
because she had once been cold, dark, and numbing and she had once known what it was to be lost before she knew what it was to be found

she said that when she was words,
when she was an ocean,
when she was a butterfly, when she was a blizzard—

she was always a dreamer
because she never stopped living
even when one life ran out of time

and i wondered if she had dreamt
a thousand lives before her or if
she had really lived so many times

and i knew she was a dreamer but she'd never lie
  about her dreams
and i thought, if she hadn't really lived all those lives
then how could she make this life so beautiful?

things left unsaid

they walked the same earth
breathed the same air
took the same path every afternoon
and then he was gone.

the trees looked empty
without him between them
the drum set looked lonely
without his guitar and

the little house
on the end of the avenue
looked sorrier than
it had ever looked

the breeze still whispered
without him
and life still went on
without him

but she never told anyone
that the night he left
she sobbed so much
she couldn't swallow her dinner

and the night he left
she wept at the moonlit sky
and knew he'd never get to see
those beautiful stars

one and a half decades
does not even begin to describe
what a young life is and
nobody ever knew

what he left unsaid
was what he took with him
and what she left unsaid
was something she'd never get to say

they'd never spoken more than one word
to each other and they had never
had the same friends or been to the same parties
or stood side by side

but once upon a time they stared
at the same stoplight and watched the same trees in autumn;
and suddenly one day he wasn't at the stoplight
and he'd never see another autumn again

lost

life is hard to beat
heartbreak kills; no one comes out
alive anyway

suspense

waiting patiently
    the clock ticks
        —without cause

misinterpretation

clouded eyes
of a girl
whose eyes see best

contradiction

oblivion,
by my standards,
does not mean
to be forgotten.

oblivion
means
your identity is lost
but your mark on the world remains.

oblivion
cannot possibly erase
the prints you made
with your footsteps

oblivion
cannot change
how different destiny would be
if you'd never interfered with fate

oblivion
can strip you of everything
but
it can't take away what's already there

oblivion
does not recognize your character
your identity, or your voice
but rather

oblivion
can erase you
but it can't
erase the evidence of you.

so are you forgotten
or are you
simply
unremembered?

bigger pictures

we are ants.
souls with no direction and hearts that are too quiet to make a sound,
scrambling over territory we know we need to share.
we are stomped on
and we can't find our way through the midday sunshine as we crawl
moving across the scalding sidewalk and beneath the cracks that we fall through
without knowing;

we are stray dogs,
walking around with no place to go, constantly searching for another scent
to sniff, wanting to find someone who can love us.

we are flowers, hiding in the dead of winter;
limp stems and shriveled petals beneath the newfallen snow.

we brave the stinging winds of dark nights and we brace ourselves
for the all too familiar cold of another tomorrow.

finally

my eyes used to be closed
against gray nights
and stomping thunder clouds.
but when i opened them,
you were standing there,
blocking the shadows.
the sun came out
and you let it beam into my eyes.
you helped me see the world
more beautifully than i ever had.
i marveled at a beautiful bird on a lilac branch
even though they said that the birds had already migrated;
i watched the last leaves fall even though they said the trees
  were all already bare;
i felt the sun on my shoulders even though they said it was
  too cold to feel it at all;
most of all, i saw everything else that was invisible
  to them,
because they tried to tell me what the world would
  look like—
but what i had not known
was that their eyes were still closed.

the luckier soul's eyes

in a slow march down the hall walked the girl in the yellow sundress next to all of the others; the girl whose footsteps were quiet and careful, and whose voice was calm and unheard. the girl whose very presence made the eyes of her watchers shine, but it was a shine that they did not notice. the girl was modest and reserved with small, shy eyes and a crooked smile, and a voice that quavered when it spoke.

she was the girl whose very eyes told a story, and perhaps the girl could be surrounded by love, but this love was one she did not get. time and time again, she silently stepped back without consideration, convincing herself that it was a love she instead did not deserve.

the other girls walked beside her triumphantly, with a poised stance that the small timid girl did not quite possess, and perhaps, she thought to herself with a frown, they were better than she ever would be. perhaps everyone surrounding her noticed her importance, but they created an illusion she had not yet detected, and the girl walked on with sorrowful eyes.

the underconfident soul stared out into the emptiness of disappointment and waited for something promising to come along and cheer her up, but when nothing came, she waited and pretended as if nothing had ever happened.

even though the tears were just on the brim of her eyelids, and her eyes grew glassy with the feeling of failure and her lips pursed with frustration, she still walked up onto the hot stage that shone bright lights on her narrow face. she walked into the crowded room filled with people—people whose minds resorted to judge her every move.

she walked past the woman in the long pink skirt and the lady in the white scarf and the man with the booming voice; and she walked beside the omnipresent alternate soul who was being praised for all of the deeds she had done, and who was being congratulated for an accomplishment she had won; the soul who received everything and who did nothing to deserve it while she sat back, watching as usual as someone with her same potential received something she knew she would never receive.

she thought to herself that perhaps someday, if she held her head high enough, that she'd wipe away the tears and see everything she had always yearned for, just as if she had been peering through the luckier soul's eyes.

opposites

i've never seen such an empty mosaic.

somber

today i heard a song in the grocery store.
it took me back to a moment i'll never forget.
i'm lying in the middle of a field
at half-past ten,
basking in the warm breeze that whispers summer
even though it is only mid-april.
i'm looking at the stars,
hidden behind thin clouds
and a deep sky
the moon made periwinkle.
we are on a big blanket we tried to stretch
to fit us all, but our feet are hanging off the edge.
we all lay close together, silent and still.
i turn on my music, a song a friend had suggested;
and everyone groans at the first chord
but after it has played through once, they ask
can you play it again? and it plays on repeat.
we huddle close and bury our heads in the blanket,
closing our eyes as it soothes us with every slow note.
we will all remember this night forever;
clear and quiet and beautiful
when we sat beneath the stars
and looked up at what was beyond our reach.
when we lay together peacefully

feeling summer winds breathe at our necks,
just barely here but still mostly gone.
when we buried our heads beneath the fleece
and the grass that smelled like dreams
and suddenly, people i had hardly known my whole life
are drawn by this moment, to my memory, my youth
and become dear to me.

bad dreams i never woke up from

- one monday at 4:42 pm
- the second week in august at a beach in a thunderstorm
- her old photographs
- a friend whose hand i never got to hold for the last time
- angered eyes and violent hands, demeaning me in
abandoned silence
- one last goodbye they tried to wait for, but came too late

my bad dreams are just a list of heartbreaks that life could not conclude.

meanings that disappear

where is the place
where old souls go?
is it on a steep riverbank
covered in snow?
is it between the scales
of a shimmering fish,
or within a magic penny
we throw to grant our wish?

where can i find love?
is it in between the raindrops
or in the call of a mourning dove?
or perhaps it is in the smiling eyes
of a grinning, joyous child
in simple surprise?

where is life's meaning
is it between our toes?
or do we sniff it without thought
like air through our nose?
does it dwell upon metallic rust?
or maybe it's in pieces and all its remnants
have faded into dust

emotional dissection

there is dark and then there is light, and then there are quiet midnights that are not bright enough to be light but not deep enough to be darkness, so they linger silently, like a soft dim glow among the other shadows.

there is hot and then there is cold and then there are crying souls with teardrops not burning enough to be hot, but not bitter enough to be cold. when they fall they are more lukewarm, like the temperature of a heart filled with burning desire as it slowly drains with each new pang of hurt; like the water feels on the seashore if you just graze your toes on the ocean water and the surface of the tide. and yet, even though they are lukewarm, the tears are hot enough to sting and cold enough to shiver and make you quiver in hushed pain while they fall uncontrollably from your eyes.

there is shiny and then there is dull and then there is glazed, which is not tasteful enough to shine but not tasteless enough to be dull. it is a glaze, like the way your eyes gleam when they grow glassy with these brimming tears, or when sadness bubbles over—but it is not permanent enough to be shiny and not absent enough to be dull. it is simply a glaze that fades after a while, like the pain that triggers those glassy eyes and just like a glaze, the pain will not last forever.

there is love and there is longing and then there is lost, which is like trying to find your way around the smallest town you've ever seen. a town you've visited thousands of times, but that you always seem to lose your way in. even though you know how to get from place to place, you still can't find the spot where you belong. and you are standing on the street, looking out at the great empty road before you and you feel so deeply alone, so utterly lost even though you are holding a map of the town right there in your very hands. but you know you are not going to stay here, and after a while you will leave and you will find familiarity again. and being lost will not feel like loss; it will just be remembered as a temporary loneliness once you feel love again. being lost does not last forever. because—

there is forever and there is never and then there is something in between. life. it has no compromise, no comparison. but between forever and never, it is full and beautiful and profound and wondrous. never may not be never, and forever may not exist, but the only place we can live in, the only compromise we know—the only compromise we'll ever know—is a compromise called time.

waking up

"we all have scars," she said
"the good and the bad."

i saw someone cry
last night in the doorway

i watched someone at school
lose fifteen pounds in thirteen days

i saw my best friend hurt herself
because she thinks it makes up for how others have hurt her

i listen to my old teacher smile
while he reads us a story that feels like he's drowning

and i've seen the trees
grow lonely in the winter

but

last night i saw someone
laugh so hard they had to stop to catch their breath.

i watched the someone heal
within the very walls of their own heart

i saw my best friend
smile despite the voices to contradict her

i listen to my old teacher
talk about the future as if its beauty lies in his hands

and i've seen the spring
bring the trees the company of new leaves

"they call the bad scars *scars*," she said,
"but you know what they call the good ones?"

"the memories," she whispered
"because there is always room for tomorrow."

new

nowhere is still somewhere
everything is still always something and
waiting is still worth it all

ten

my

world

is

yours

too;

now

i

know

about

peace

trapped

last night was a nightmare i do not wish to return to, for she was standing in front of me, covered by a white sheet. it draped around her thin and bony shoulders and wrinkled in a heap at her feet. she stood, staring into the wall before her, and revealing nothing about herself but the dark curls that fell upon her back.

she whispered so softly to me; in a voice so frightened and alone. she shivered so that i could not make out the words; and the words she feared the most surrounded her in writing and in voice. they were written on the wall and on the sheet and across her back and at her feet and contradictions nestled in her hair.

her tiny screams were drowned by the silence of the enclosed room, but her thoughts echoed through my mind. though now she was silent, i could hear her cries loudest now; and i shook with her pain. suddenly her emotion was mine and it was red hot and stinging and it surged through my veins and filled my eyes with tears.

i was captured by their never ceasing criticism, and their demeaning stares; and the commands they threw at me and waited for me to catch, as if i were there just to please them. as if my life were a small bird they wished to hold captive in their hands long enough to hope i had forgotten how to fly.

this is not about you

i'm sure you knew exactly what the future looked like, it just felt better to look in the opposite direction. i used to want to blame myself because you'd claimed i had blocked your view, but then i realized you'd *told* me to stand there because you thought my hair looked pretty reflecting the sun and you wanted to take a picture. i used to want to be offended when you burned that picture as soon as you saw how it turned out, but then i realized it wasn't because of how i looked in the light, it was because you didn't want to pay attention to the bigger pictures you saw being taken in the distance.
i used to want to believe you, but then i realized you didn't want to be honest because you were too afraid it could
kill you.

and then i realized i'd be the one dead if i kept waiting for the truth. i used to have more than one chance, but i think that was the only one that mattered—especially when you told me i had used them all up.

observations

somewhere else in the world—
it's either yesterday or tomorrow

rain is heavy enough
to bend marble gravestones

black and white don't belong
in a rainbow but they look beautiful together

once upon a time one person
didn't know what music was until they made it

destiny doesn't have time to make us
second-guess ourselves

balloons always end up
popping somewhere in the distant sky

it's never been established
that there is just one universe

and

life is always the cause of death.

in our last days

when we grow old and look back on our youth,
we won't remember what grade the biology teacher gave us at
the end of the semester
or what color shoes we were wearing on the first day
of kindergarten

we won't remember the things we thought we'd remember
fifty years ago, and maybe we'll remember the things
we never thought to think about

like the smell of freshly baked cookies on a rainy day
or the lullaby we fell asleep to every night
or the way it felt to make a new friend on the playground

we won't remember all the friends we aged with,
but we'll remember the ones we aged without
and how we never got to give them a proper goodbye that
could hold on long enough

we won't remember what night it was or even what month
but we'll remember someday that once, we were young
enough
to fit on one picnic blanket and watch the stars together
at midnight

we won't remember when curfew was or even how old
we were
but we'll remember someday that once, we were young
enough
to light off fireworks past dusk and still get scolded for being
out too late

i used to hate getting in trouble because it made me
imperfect
i used to hate being vulnerable because it made me real, but
someday i'll miss being yelled at for lighting fireworks
outside with my friends past dusk

and watching stars at midnight

would it be enough?

if i believed
your sugar-coated words
and wove my way into
your perfect world
would you be happy?

if i jumped high enough
to touch your flawless blue sky
painted thinly on a white canvas
with watercolor
would you be satisfied?

if i closed my eyes
and pretended to capture
the wisdom you wish to possess,
and i recognized your every pride
would you be at peace?

if i bowed at your feet
and granted your every wish, without fail
without complaint, until i rotted
in the mess of your past and the mistakes you made
would you love me?

but
if i held your gaze
long enough to reveal
that your soul is shallow and transparent
and i walked away,
do you think you could do without me?

the layers of us

everyone has an outside and an inside. the outside is what we prefer people to see; it is the version of ourselves that we're a little less ashamed of, slightly more confident with. it's the one part of us that we can show to others. i think many of us keep the outside minimal compared with what goes on in the inside. it's been established that people are great at hiding things, but i don't think we are hiding them as much as keeping them from view. we are beginning to split our soul into two layers—the one that can be seen and the one that can't. from day one, it's been the way we do things.

no matter how confident, how social, how personable, how comfortable someone is—they still have an element unseen. there is the layer beneath the outer one. the inside of our soul is the solid core, the place you have to dig deepest to find. its shell is titanium, perfect silver metal, shiny and so admirable it's untouchable. we think the titanium is the most amazing part; the last thing there is to unearth. but if you look close enough, the titanium is thin enough to see through.

we all have it—another layer beneath what others seem to think is the core. some people don't care enough to break through the titanium because they find it too hard a task, but others see that really, it's not titanium at all—and they peel away at it as if it is as easy as tearing tin foil.

there aren't too many people like that in the world, but you have to find them—it's as easy as that. it's not the fault of people for not wanting to dissolve the titanium and see what's underneath. we have to make them understand that our shell is paper-thin, and it's a wall waiting to be broken through at any second. we need to relieve our fear of being known from the inside and decide that the real version of ourselves isn't anything to be ashamed of.

self-consciousness is an illusion, because we base what we think we should be according to what others appear to be. but if we all cracked open our shells and shone from the inside, there would be no comparison of our light versus anyone else's—it would all be beautifully different, gloriously unique.

so why can't we, as a people, crack open our shells altogether and close our eyes, and open our real souls on a count of three? how much easier would it be, then, to find peace within ourselves?

rare instances

i screamed to the stars
on a moonlit night,
a song of anger
and of madness so right
it felt wrong

dreaming

i guess maybe, after a while,
i was just so lost
that when i closed my eyes
my subconscious
was still wrapped up in the very miracle of you

and i guess maybe, after a while,
it will be a little further
in the past
and i'll stop feeling so lonely
when i remember
that you always used to be beside me

i guess maybe, after a while
when i smiled in my sleep
and my thoughts wandered
to imaginary realities, i guess
i woke up. but you weren't there
to tell me i was dreaming

like you used to
when i shook with fear
and you held me close
and whispered, “it’s okay.
i’ll always be here for you.”
and i squeezed your hand, and said, “me, too.”

colors and math

we see life in rainbows
but sometimes we just don't realize quite how brilliant
that is.

how wonderful would life be
if people stopped pretending that rainbows only have two
colors—the one they fight for, and the one they do not?

life is endlessly beautiful, but sometimes we pretend there are
only two sides
the side of winning, and the side of not.

the truth is there is always something more to fight for.
the other side of winning is not losing; and winning is not
everything.

yes, there are only two sides of the number line—negative
and positive
but there are infinite numbers between.

stereotypes

when can people be introverts without
being antisocial? and when can
men paint their nails without being
called gay? when can girls stop being
blamed for rape, just because
they weren't sober enough to fight someone
who already should've respected *NO*
in the first place? when can feminism
stop being mistaken for war? and when
will people start to root for humanity?

i'd like to know why people think
depression can be cured with a
"better attitude" and i'd like to think
that anxiety is more powerful than
something you can "just get over" and
i'd like to imagine a world where
the color of your skin doesn't change
the justice you deserve; a world where people
will stop being afraid of who they are

why do people spend so much time
asking themselves why they aren't
good enough and why do people
joke about suicide when they

know it will never be funny? when can
girls walk down the street without
being pawed at by greed and profanity? when
can people stop facing fear for loving
someone of the same sex and when
will everyone else accept that love is love?

if we could witness ourselves jump
to countless conclusions and make
so many generalizations, when would
we admit it's all for nothing? judging
will never change the world, it will just
add to its suffering and when will we be
old enough to grow up? so many people
pass through a lifetime of experience
and still don't understand

that we are all just people

amazement

i don't know
why,
but when i stared into your
eyes
i was home again, back to
long
beautiful summers and sweltering heat,
to
the innocence i left just as soon as i
had
acquired it

love's paradox

gone are the days of carelessness, when careful is safe and danger is miles away from reach; gone is the faith that our dreams are our virtue.

we are people of a society subject to judgment, an experiment of youth and damage and emotion, and as we learn we are hurt too often for our own good. we wish we weren't in our own skin; wish, for a million different reasons, that we could be perfect, and we consume ourselves so hopelessly trying to match up to everything we expected ourselves to be when we cannot believe in reality.

we are exhausted, suffocating in the hate of our enemies and the criticism of those whose opinions we regard the most; we are tired of the tireless competition of whose life is worse or better when no one can win this battle.

it's a hard truth to face when our souls bleed each and every single doubt, and our eyes are vacant with the emptiness that we gain each time a renewed spark of promise leaves us.

we are the future of the world, the generations of realizations that judgment from others defines us, that their disapproval is what makes us, that we should lose all hope when it is lost the first time. our hearts are scarred with rejection and sorrow and the love we've always wished for, but never had.

someday we can unite to find that the hope we once possessed is all that matters in knowing where we stand with our dreams; and the belief that faith exists is a simple state of mind that we need to enter again to regain our consciousness—of who we are, why we're here, and the purpose of our existence.

when all you shed are tears that are the shattered glass of dreams ruined by someone else, wipe them away and throw out the shards so you'll never get cut by them again. the impression of their footprints inside your heart can easily be brushed away, so dust yourself off and let your heart find a new song, one they fear to even begin to violate. don't let the judgment stomp all over you, because one day you will be big enough to stand up; but when you do, don't use your strength to stomp on them.

shake hands and stare into the eyes of the enemy long enough to realize that regardless of whatever reputation we've gotten, or success or punishment we have received, we are all just people, citizens of this world, all trying to do the right thing, pushing through the crowd for a desperate chance to stand up and use our voice. each of us aspiring that one day maybe the passion that we foster every single day can one day be enough to change the world.

but maybe the kind of security—the love we have spent our whole lives searching for until our eyes are dark and tired, and our hearts are raw and hopeless from fighting against what everyone else believes—is not what we're really looking for.

fatigued

listening
    for a silence
that won’t arrive

suicide note

i tried to listen for the birds to chirp or the leaves to rustle or the wonderful hymn of midsummer cicadas to let me know he was still there. but he wasn't. i was listening for a sign that he was still talking, still trying to scramble through his words to find something that would explain exactly what he meant by *this is all too much*. i really never guessed it would take me this long to recover and that four months later, i'd still be watching the lake stand still in december and wonder if the reason it hasn't snowed yet is because it was already cold enough last summer, and the clouds are still frozen in shock.

he meant his last letter to be a reason, an explanation, but i don't think he was ever really telling the truth. i don't think he ever got to bottom of what was bothering him because he was too scared to uncover it, and maybe that's what really made him want to give up. he's so gone now it's hard for me to even think of a time when he was happy, but i guess that's just part of losing someone. i know i don't grieve like you do. but i grieve.

Dear Friend,
You are the one who will read this when I am long gone. I know you found this because you always knew where I hid my secrets. I'm assuming you think this is just another one of them, but the truth is, it isn't. It was never a secret that I was too scared to live

any longer or that my mind was too messed up to keep going. I know you told me so many times that you'd be there for me, and I feel utterly horrible for saying this, but I don't think it was ever enough unless I knew you could make the pain go away. Some of us are stronger than we seem, and others are weaker than we seem. I am the latter. I hide in the fire escape of my uncle's apartment and the balcony of my grandmother's house when I paint the sunset. They used to be an escape and now they're just getaways. People want to believe escape and get away mean the same thing, but they don't. I needed an escape that would last forever, and I don't want you to bother coming to find me, though I will always hold you dear to my heart.

This is all too much. I give you my deepest apologies.

his name was scrawled in blue ink at the bottom of the page, his signature. he had written the note in perfect punctuation, perfect grammar, perfect togetherness, but i never saw it as enough; the longest note in the world, the best explanation in the world, could never do justice to a life that precious. that was the day i left it in my desk at work and you took it out and scribbled out his name to write yours. one over another. one after the other.

i know i don't grieve like you do. but i grieve.

irony

they say
that color
adds energy to life

then why
must they be violent
beholding it?

they say that color
is beautiful and appreciated
then why must they shame diversity?

they say
that without color
life would be black and white,

and i say
isn't that what they want?

thorns

i grew upon careful soil
sprouted from a perfect seed;
round with beauty and with
blooming life.

i grew until my leaves swelled
with radiance,
until my petals blushed
in beauty;

until my vines knotted,
entwined around
a chainlink fence that
i used to stay straight

they came out every afternoon
at half past two to visit me;
to sniff my petals and marvel
at my delicacy.

and one, bursting with curiosity,
wished to touch my fragile stem;
and though warned, reached out—
and i stung him with my thorns.

i was born with thorns.
the rest of the roses, too, not by choice
but by nature; though still, now, they act as if
i chose to hurt them.

they no longer came to tend to me;
not to water, not to smell,
not even to bask in the summer sunshine.
and i was lonely under pale skies.

my petals wilted
in hopeless despair
and in great fear that they
would never come back

i bathed in raindrops
in damp soil and frozen tears
and i swayed beneath the clouds
until i gathered strength again

but even with pink glow
and the admirable beauty
i had always wished for—
they never once stopped to look at me.

to hurt is to suffer

do not waste your hurting
by dismissing it.

do not ignore your feelings,
the way they dread.

let your heart pour out
everything it's got

let it give away one shattered piece
for just one night

enough for you to know
it is strong enough to leave the pieces it doesn't need

because
they are just evidence

testifying
for a heartbreak you'll never want to remember again

so let them bleed and know
that your heart will fill with love

and become whole again;
someday

choices

i like the blue but
she told me i should wear green
because it brings out my eyes

too late

i once saved a monarch with two broken wings…

the very same window

i visited you nine times.

1. i look at you. you look straight back at me and give me an admirable reflection to marvel at.
2. you look at me again, but i don't see the same reflection. you adorn my jawline with the rainbow beams of sunshine that stray from your shining glass.
3. you are wet from the rain. droplets are still leftover from last night's storm. my eyes look larger than usual in the raindrops.
4. you are steamy from the sun. too much rain this season has brought you to steam up every single time a puddle melts into the sweltering air.
5. you are frosty from the autumn. when i was little, i used to think jack frost visited you every single time i walked by and saw the beautiful patterns of white etched into your glass, but you just tell me it bothers you to tolerate them now.
6. one unbearable blizzard has frozen you so much you crack. at first you apologize, and tell me it makes you look unflattering, but i tell you one flaw won't change how you reflect in the sunshine. i don't tell you that my reflection looks a little different now that you aren't whole anymore.

7. i come back to look at you again in the spring. you cry about how you can't peer through to observe the blooming flowers and the freshly laid mulch anymore because you've cracked again. spring's unavoidable hail has given you spiderweb-like lines.
8. you say you don't know how much more of this you can take. you're thankful when a warning comes out that they're tearing your building down to remodel a new one. i say goodbye to you.
9. the last time i saw you, you were shattering to the concrete floor. you lay in millions of pieces. i remember when you were new, but i suppose you can't stay new forever. they sweep up your shards and bring your remains to a truck. i watch it drive away.

where you used to be, there's a skyway.

bittersweet

the saddest and most regretful part, perhaps,
of not cherishing being young
or of wishing you still were,
is that when you were small
all you wanted to do was grow up
and when you were little
you pranced around in "big kid" clothes, not knowing what
growing up meant after all

dirty dishes

the counter is a mess
of bread crumbs and butter.

the water's still boiling
in the pot on the stove;

her cookbook is still open
to page 68

and the phone is ringing
because she forgot to call her mother.

she ran to the basement to get ice for the freezer
and now she is so frozen she will never come back

but there are still numbers on the fridge
she hasn't yet called

and a mug in the microwave
of coffee that has now grown cold

the biggest knife
is missing from the drawer

and there are still dirty dishes in the sink
that she will never clean

hope

it's not too late
to discern that
the dark is just
an illusion

false

in school when i was taught about consent
i learned it was about a female giving a male permission.

consent is not just about a female giving
a male permission

it is an agreement between two parties
rather than just one

a male can say no just the same as
a female can

because no one wants to be used
or treated as if they were useless

we are demeaning ourselves by pretending
that a female is always the one to say no

we are demeaning ourselves by pretending
that a male is always the instigator

we are demeaning ourselves by pretending
love can only exist between a male and female

we need to change the way we teach our children
about consent, and about the way love exists

consent is an agreement between two people
even when they think they already know the answer

and love is a bond between two people whose hearts
speak to one another, no matter who they are

it's not just black and white
it's a rainbow

and it's not just one story
it's a two-way street

it can even be something as simple as asking
at the stoplight if you should keep driving

and turning around when your friend
says they want to go home instead

friendship

where had the time gone at 2 a.m.
when i was standing in front of you
telling you how valued you are
in a world full of skepticism? i guess
time had fled the last time you
stood in front of me and told me
that i am important no matter what
and you finally got through to me—enough
for me to love you enough
to get through to you. and
i didn't care what the clock said i just
cared that you stayed around long enough
to be reminded that i'd wait until the *end*
of time if it meant more time for you

alibi

she was at the park when he was shot
and his mother was in the kitchen

his brother was at hockey practice during his death
and his mother was making dinner

his friend was at the movies when he perished
and his mother was setting the table

his father was at work when his wife called in tears
but his mother was finally alone.

four little words

"it is no secret—"
what? you were honest!
"please listen to me."
no. (and hung up)
"wait, i'll be there."

two painful fights later:
"the stars are aligned!"
you would tell me,
"this is so beautiful."

after a quiet dinner,
"where is the receipt?"
i lost it, but
"yes, i forgive you."
thank you. thank you.

"we both made mistakes."
i see it now.
"give me a chance?"
i'm not so sure.
"you are so perfect…"
no, neither are you.

"i'm sorry, it's over."
comes out of nowhere
"i'm sorry i lied."
doesn't make sense

"it hurts me too..."
you said, and cried.
"i am almost gone."
you said, and left.

"...regret to inform you..."
their words a blur
"write about me someday."
your four last words

the truth

it's so sugar-coated that i feel claustrophobic.

questions

if happy *endings* exist,
then why can we believe
our spirit lives on—if
there is no end?

isn't it just the happy moments
that prolong
our memory?

we say these things and
we may never know

but why pretend?

small talk

your idea of small talk is
discussing why mountains get confused with volcanoes
sharing conspiracies of the day JFK died
pondering the way our life would turn out if we could take
back one wrong decision
asking me to explain everything about my life that i have
ever been disappointed by
and asking me to recollect everything else that has ever made
me happy
bringing me a new memory to replace all the things i
have lost
demanding each small detail when you ask me how my
day was
listening when i describe each and every dream i live for
asking me what i want to name my dog in fifteen years and
having a conversation about all the things we've ever
encountered that don't seem to add up

you've never asked me about the weather
or accepted a one-word adjective in response when you ask
me how i am doing
you have never tried to get to know me by talking
about sports
or my favorite things

you just took enough time to ask the questions that mattered
and you found my soul within every answer and
  every hesitation
without even asking me what my favorite color was
or what i had for dinner last night

you think about what matters and you dig for it.
you don't just give up when someone is quiet
you don't need the temporary things, because you are the
  first person to understand
that there are smaller things that matter more
and that is only one of the things i love most about you.

mirror

he stood in the mirror...
admired his reflection.

there is more to be done
and still yet to learn

he smiles at his friends
leaves school forty minutes late

and this isn't the first time
he's been heartbroken

but what is heaven without the living?

he's been heartbroken
and this isn't the first time

leaves school forty minutes late
he smiles at his friends

and still yet to learn
there is more to be done

admired his reflection.
he stood in the mirror...

alternate realities

we were
a masterpiece
painted with gold
but instead now i'm just a
painting you stole

we were
a wonderfully
innocently
assembled melody
before you erased the notes

unfathomable things

too often, my brain tries
to stretch itself across
things that are too big
to wrap any mind around

like the universe, in its
ever-dynamic restlessness
makes my heart sleepless
itching to know of its creation

before us, there was earth
and before earth, our galaxy
and before our galaxy, the universe
but tell me, what came before that?

in chronological order, you
can separate science and reality
and deduce your theories to proof
but

no matter what we've proven
there is no evidence of how
our whole universe
came to be

and it would appear that
it all burst out of a nothingness
but if that is true, then where
did the nothingness begin?

clarify

it may seem as though
i write when i am unhappy

but the truth is that i write
whenever i am inspired

my inspiration can come
from any emotion;

but it must have the fire in me
that compels me before i can write.

my words may appear
harsh, or sorrowful;

but the truth is that i use deep emotion—
not sadness—to tell my story

i have had high and low moments
here and there, everywhere

i witness the sorrow of others
and i write about their story

i grieve
and i write about my emotions

i feel a high of happiness wash over me
and i write about the moments

i change the names and disguise
the themes

because writing is all about
being creative

it may seem as though i write
about a specific time, or a specific *someone*

yes. often. though not always;
because

words, however simple,
are never what they seem.

angry

why did you think you could do that to me? to anyone?
no one ever told you it was okay
to use someone for anything other than
being human. no one ever told you it was okay
to give a girl the respect of a toy—and not
the kind of toy you sew back together and
cuddle up with at night; the kind of toy
you throw in a closet, let it gather with dust
and never look back.

who told you it was all right?
or did anybody even mind to give approval?
did you ask for anyone's advice, or did you
just not care enough?
or did you just not want to hear
the answer? where are your boundaries? and
where is your conscience? did someone stop
you, or did you walk away before they could?
did someone stop you, or did you ignore them?

i would never suck up to you enough
to actually walk up and ask these questions
myself, but i wish you had enough of a mind
to know that these are the questions you should
be asking yourself before you decide to treat

someone as if they are worthless. these
are the questions you should be asking yourself
before you decide to forget it all and leave someone
to suffer in the dark and cold memory of what you did.

destinations

where were you when you had your first heartbreak?
the peak of age fifteen

where were you when you made your first fried egg?
the kitchen of my mother's old house at three

where were you when you found out the first loss you'd
grieve was gone?
in the garden of lilacs where my sister was wed

where were you when you first felt guilt tug away at
your heart?
in the middle of a fight with my childhood best friend

and where were you when you ran away?
i was in no place to explain

competition

too often, i see us
view life as a competition.
i see us yearning for power
and losing our souls to get it;
i see us wearing our hearts
on our sleeve, just to prove
that we have it harder than
everyone else; and i see us,
crying because we believe we
are not good enough, simply
because we listened to another
who is just as insecure.

i see that we trip people just
because it satisfies us to be the
first to the finish line; and really
we don't stop to see if they are
okay, even when we win. i see
that we sometimes criticize the way people
try to push for equality, simply
because some people view the
battle for equality as a competition
for who is better or worse. but what
we don't see is so many people
who have felt so worthless for so long

it does not mean that we want
power, or victory, or praise, and it
does not mean we want more or
less than what anyone else already has;
we just want validation, no matter
what our position in society portrays; and
i think deep down, regardless of who we are,
all of us sometimes feel as if we are broken,
and we don't want to compete with anyone,
or be the best at anything;
we just want to feel that our worth is the same

as anyone else's

dialogue

but you promised,
she murmured
to the memory of him standing in front of her

a promise is just a word,
he insisted, *because who*
could ever guarantee
something so timeless?

she took a deep breath;
tried not to cry; closed her eyes
and said
i could.

explaining color to someone without sight

what is color? i'm sure you've heard of the word before—of course, it seems foreign to you, and you are ever curious of its meaning. people tell you color is the sensation you get when looking at something that portrays a certain shade or tint, a certain amount of light or darkness. they tell you color is incredible; it paints itself ombré patterns in summer sunsets and illustrates its beauty in art and allows us to see through someone's soul when we stare at the brilliant blue of their eyes. it weaves in and out of wool blankets and curls up in the worn pocket of last year's purple raincoat. it turns our knuckles white with fear and flashes through our cheeks in times of anger. color splashes sense into the world and depicts the future in abstract ways. it hides under red umbrellas in the rain and dries up in the yellow sunshine as it stings our eyes. color is everywhere.

but color is everywhere.

color is the shade of our skin. the reason why people hide at night for fear of blame due to their race; the reason why people are shot dead without justice done to their ever pleading innocence; the reason why so many of us walk around amid the reality of discrimination. color is the reason why we haven't lived in peace yet. the reason why we still fear its deep red when we glance down at our wounds.

it's the trail of blood after a war that we can't erase. color is the absence of itself in transparent tears and pain we carry behind our waiting eyes. color is the dispute between pink and blue that ignited a war between the sexes. color is everywhere.

color is how we tell fruits are ripe; if not to our satisfaction, we don't take them. color is how we waste a life every time someone wants white meat instead of red. color is how we decipher whether to stop or whether to go; it is how we decide what flowers to pick and which ones are already brown and shriveled. color is everything, and color is nothing.

is it hard to be absent of sight? not to know how color appears? and if i couldn't see your orange walking stick, i'd never know your eyes were any different than mine. i'd never know the color of your skin, or that you can't see in the same way that i can. i could only hear your voice. melodious. and kind. if i couldn't see, i'd never know. what if the whole world were blind? what then? what if the whole world couldn't see your walking stick or my ugly scar? what then? what if that girl wasn't being teased over there because of her face? what if hundreds of lives could be saved without the perception of color? what then?

i stare at you, watch you listen to me explore a plethora of possibilities. but you can't see my tears when it hits me. you can't even see transparency; you can only hear the sound of my pain. and i watch you for a moment, still and silent and beautiful. even if i couldn't see you, your quiet thought would still be one of the most beautiful things i have ever witnessed.

i close my eyes, hear your soft breathing and listen to your gentle response.

maybe the whole world is blind. maybe all we see is darkness because it hurts to stare at the light sometimes, just like staring into the sun on a hot day, but if we didn't have the sun, how would we stay warm? we just don't see enough, like we should. things look larger when you put them in a glass of water, but really we're staring right through their colorlessness, just like we do everything else. the worst thing about seeing color is seeing the absence of it.

i can see. i can see color.

but you can see far more than i ever will.

time

well, when i was small,
it was so far from reach that i hardly knew it existed
and now, it is so apparent
it's hard to remember anything else.

traveler's sorrow

voices call to me, half-asleep
trying to find their purpose
and vanish the guilt behind their name

their frozen eyes crack
and their teardrops linger like icicles

as they bathe in the raindrops
and fall with the snow,
i follow the highway
by the sunset's golden glow

a traveler by night
a mourner by day;
i watch the hearts they take for granted
shatter to shards

post-its

the first of the pack:
oranges
mangoes
peaches
hummus
a few coconut waters for the road
potato chips
twizzlers
no-bake cheesecake
yogurt (but not vanilla)

more demands:
write Language Arts essay in time for friday deadline
practice new cello music
turn in algebra homework—otherwise no A
don't forget about homecoming dance on saturday

goodbye wishes:
finish poems
get a pedicure
get a new haircut
pack for college
play your favorite sonata on the grand piano one last time before you leave. kiss the keys with your fingertips.

out-of-style notes:
buy cake for daughter's birthday
don't forget the dentist appointment for thursday
write get-well card for father—death is hard to brave
stop writing these to-do lists on post-its. she says it's inconvenient.

last-minute thoughts:
when i was a girl
i used to write instead of type
encouragements
to-do lists
and spur-of-the-moment poetry
so don't throw this away
yet

old friends

i bet you don't remember
that before we were born
iphones did not exist.

the first words i heard
escape from her mouth
when i saw her again after thirty-five years

i bet you had forgotten
that i have a picture of us at ten
wearing athletic shorts over our leggings

my response to her
is a memory i had imagined
had left her mind too

i don't know if you can imagine it,
but when we were in the sixth grade
we tried to sneak our makeup to school

she urges me to
dig in the depths of my soul
and find that beautiful innocence

i know we are older now,
but i can still recollect all of the times
we were too engulfed by time to know we were young

i whisper,
and she frowns
and stares at me

i can hardly fathom a time when
our biggest priorities were secrets
and hiding our list of code names

she says, and
we sit there for a moment; breathe,
say in soft voices, in eerie togetherness—

i am sorry we grew apart
though time didn't allow us to stay; and i'm sorry
we forgot what it was like to fly away

what beauty feels like

beauty feels like
fireworks through my veins
like hearing a song and loving it so much that you
turn the music all the way up, roll the windows down, and
stick out your arm
with the wind in your hair

beauty feels like
my soul is weightless
flying on golden wings and loving it so much that i
feel free, all over, in every way that could possibly be

beauty feels like
a summer night in the heat of july
like looking up at the night sky and its endless wonder
and never wanting this moment to end

beauty feels
effortless, soaring, and fleetingly
magical, so vividly exhilarating
that it is beyond articulation

broken hourglass

back before she had a watch
she used an hourglass to tell time
until one day in burning rage
she threw time away

its remains were in millions
of shards and wedges of glass
grains of glittering sand
and she threw time away

what had she been thinking before she found out that time
persists no matter how many times it's thrown away?

falling behind

chasing cars
with my eyes;
too fast to follow

love letter

i don't think i ever knew you well enough to be friends. it seemed like your rainstorm of emotions was enough to drown a whole city. i wouldn't touch something so destructive with a ten-foot pole. i guess you could say i never really burned enough to share your fire, but maybe i just gave you oxygen instead. you never loved me, and i never loved you, but we never hated each other either. i think we just enjoyed each other's presence because it was easy and no one else understood.

i haven't seen you in years, but maybe that doesn't matter. maybe it isn't the thought that counts with you; maybe it's the actual tears you never cried. i suppose maybe i never gave you enough time to kill me, but i didn't want to perish so young. i just barely got away through a door you thought you'd locked before i turned the open knob and ran out fast enough to close it behind me. you were too smart to follow my footsteps.

it never really made sense to me why you thought your magic tricks were anything but deceit. once upon a time i thought you put on a wonderful show but then i discovered—you put on a wonderful *show*. i was looking for reality and you were looking for something temporary, but i guess in a sense they could've been the same concept. you never had the heart to amaze me and i never had the courage to admit i was scared.

i guess you could summarize it all by saying that we wanted different things out of life, however similar they were. my eyes were closed the whole time and you just blinked halfway. i couldn't see what was in front of me and you couldn't see what was far in the distance. i made enough of a sacrifice trying to decide how much i really knew you.

that was the day i ran away and we ended things before it could get worse.

that was the day i watched the rain outside of a coffee shop window and sat alone with my iced tea while i wrote a makeshift love letter on a yellow napkin.

desperation

there is
no room to breathe
but i still
haven't run out of oxygen

i can't decide whether
i'd rather suffocate in the water
or die
trying to reach the surface

censored

two parents and a child—
it's that simple.

thirteen years of school
and the option for at least four more.

someone makes dinner
before seven o'clock

and you are afraid of the dark
because the monsters could catch you.

playdates are organized
without your effort

and you can play outside until
you smell like the campfire

i don't think you ever thought
about war or peace

or the struggle to achieve
what we think is our purpose

or the agony of trying to pursue
a life when we're hitting so many obstacles

people got married in castles
in the movies

and everyone lived happily ever after
but only until they're all grown up

and you see how complicated
it all is

and it's beautiful and unobtainable and drastic
and not at all simple

indecisive

where were you
when i was aching
and you told me
you would never
be so temporary
as to leave my side?

a word for the between

when i was tiny, i used to think it was all too simple. there was life, and there was death.

when i was six, i learned of a man who had fallen into a freezing lake in the middle of winter. he had suffered from severe hypothermia and been declared dead at 3:54 am at the hospital eleven miles from his boat.

the next morning, the man was alive. his family said it was a miracle. at 7:22 am his purple lips had filled with a warm red color. the doctors said that he had been dead just short of three and a half hours. he had actually come back to life, as he seemed to thaw away the evidence that he had been dead in that hospital room.

my mother told me that this man was not the first person to be declared dead and then be revived.

when i was ten, i could not fathom how someone could come back from the dead. the meaning of death, i had thought, was being lifeless beyond revival.

when i was twelve, i learned in sixth-grade science class about why leaves changed in the winter. i learned about chlorophyll and how the trees lose their chlorophyll in the autumn and turn thin and crispy without their full green color, and eventually fall off of the trees.

the teacher asked us to make a chart of all living things and decide which category they go under: *dead or alive*. there was no in between, we decided. but then he asked us where trees in the autumn would go in the chart.

we couldn't decide. some of us argued that trees were still living in the winter and some argued that they weren't because they didn't blossom. they were just bare, empty branches burdened by snow. if they had appeared that way in the spring, they would've looked dead for sure.

my teacher told us about the word *dormant*. it meant that the trees weren't dead, but they weren't necessarily living, either. they were alive, but they weren't growing. the teacher told us about volcanoes. some were dormant. they weren't erupting, but it wasn't that they would never erupt again. they were inactive for a temporary amount of time, however long that period of time was.

that's when i learned that trees could be mistaken for dead in the winter and volcanoes could be mistaken for inactive when they didn't erupt. and i realized that neither was true. they were just dormant, and people don't think of that.

i also realized that human lives do not typically have a stage of dormancy. but i thought about the man who came back from the dead, and again i thought that if he were dead, he'd never have been able to come back to life. science would probably contradict me. but maybe he was one of those people who had a stage in his life where he was dormant, too. inactive for a temporary amount of time. alive, but not growing.

and i knew he wasn't the only one who had that kind of stage in his lifetime. it's like when your heart skips a beat, maybe you are dormant for even just a split-second because in that moment, you are not in sync with life.

maybe the notion that humans are never dormant is misleading. i am not a scientist, and i am not a doctor.

but when i was twelve, that was the only way it made sense.

if you ever read this

i hope someday you'll know
i loved you more than i could articulate
in a way i had never been able
to describe in my own words;

i hope someday you'll read
through my regretful thoughts
and finally know that i had never
wanted this to come to an end

i was scared, i guess, because
i thought if i held on too long
that it would become too temporary,
my worst fear

and i was afraid, i suppose, because
i thought if i let my heart
become one with yours, i would never
get the chance to find out what mine sounded like cn its own

but some days i try to listen
and all i can hear is the soft silence
of how lonely my heart is
without yours beside it
and when i taste the distance between us

freshly, like ocean air after a hurricane—
my heart, i hope you know
it's broken

and i have never felt more empty
than i did when we fell away
and if i could rewind, i know i'd tell myself
that we fit like puzzle pieces

i hope you remember that both of us
were broken once upon a time
but i have never felt more whole
than i did when i found you

and i'll never make you feel
anything less than whole
again; because you aren't temporary.
we were infinite.

anonymous

i would not have known
i was standing on a gravestone
if i had not noticed numbers beneath my feet.

i glanced down to see
a lifetime was curiously scrawled
in ancient granite, four tiny letters, and no name above it

dear and beloved
was the only evidence to suggest
that this person even had a known identity at all

some of the headstones
were worn by the rain and snow
that had faded their letters over the decades;

but this one was much too simple
and it was far too empty, and far too lonely;
and i knew that your name hadn't disappeared. they had just
never written it.

wonders of the mind

isn't there a time when you get tired of being sad?
when your heart is tired of beating only for existence and
not for life;
when your soul is already dead enough to be gone.
don't you get tired of hanging on by a thread
and wishing away all of your moments to leave your clouded
illusions?

i know i get tired
of pretending that smiling equals happiness
or that laughing means carelessness
or that dismissing reality is ever worth it

someday i hope you realize
how strong you are
and you laugh because you're content
instead of trying to drown your cries
and you smile because you can't
contain your happiness; not because
you need to contain your tears

twelve-word summaries

you were always my best memory,
even in the worst of times

depression's scent

people have established,
over the years
that depression is
slow, minor-key music
to the hopeless ears.

they've established
it resides
within twisting branches
and dark forests of the mind
and devouring tides.

people have established,
with great certainty
that it feels rough
with sharp edges
in its jagged asymmetry

people have described,
so meticulously
that it tastes like dried blood,
black licorice,
and mystery.

but have you ever heard them
describe its foul scent?
like bubbling gases
and dry smoke
with cruel intent

much like the smell
of a brave odor
finding its way through
your heart's
every corridor

you've heard them describe
how it vanishes a laugh
looks like a blade
and sounds like a haunted orchestra, but
have you ever heard them say its musty smell makes
  you cough?

and no one expected its
scent to be
so utterly deadly;
no one expected that even though you don't mean to
inhaling it is so toxic it could kill you

escape

if she'd known that this beautiful melody was so relieving,
why had she never sung it before?

and if you knew it was there somewhere, on the edge of what
we deem impossible, would you chase it?

heart-to-heart

i've never felt sorry for you, but i have always hurt for you. i believe there is a difference between the two because one is formed from guilt and made of sympathy, and one is formed from honest emotions and made of love. i haven't hurt for you in a way that makes me fall weak at the knees and crouch down and beg for you in the rain, but i've hurt for you in a way that makes all of the times you've ever hurt relevant to all the times i've ever hurt. it's like i understand you in a way that connects our hearts.

of course, we've never *been* hurt the same way, but we're only connected because we *hurt* the same way—we suffer the same way, ponder outcomes in the same way, wonder what's wrong with us to make us hurt this way, take it all so personally. i've never come up with enough strength to write you an apology because up until now i had thought you knew enough of this, and up until now i didn't think i needed to write you something for you to understand.

i know now that not everything comes naturally to everyone and sometimes even our strongest feelings don't come across the way we intend. maybe you don't get that love is a two-way street, and that love doesn't always need to be felt with desire. sometimes the strongest love just comes from two soul mates who love each other because their hearts beat to the same rhythm. love is mind-opening and beautiful and unlike anything else, and in all of its brilliance, it can be anything it wants. it can be exhibited in all ways, felt in all ways, formed in all ways.

i think the reason i've written this to you is because you believe in love, but you don't believe that the love people feel might not always be felt or exhibited in the way you expect it to be. i think that makes you upset, but i can't change that for you. i can't change the way you think or learn, but i can tell you this: it's worth more than you perceive it to be worth.

i'm not apologizing to you because i feel sorry for you, or because the fault falls at someone's feet. i'm apologizing because i know what you've suffered, and i can feel the way you blame yourself. it is heartbreaking that you don't see how strongly you've affected everyone who knows you for who you are.

the fact that you do not understand how grateful we all are, how grateful *i* am, to know someone as lovely as you upsets me; and maybe it upsets me because maybe i've never said it enough to ring true. but i'm saying it now in the most earnest way possible, and i hope you take enough time to listen. it will never be too late.

war

our greatest paradox
is the way we battle mercilessly
and justify it by saying that we fight for peace

because

if we were fighting for peace
we really wouldn't
be fighting at all

some advice

the next time you have a choice of whether or not
to look someone in the eye and be honest
or whether to lie to get a better reaction,
remember what it's like when the lie is uncovered
and hurts everyone who was fooled
by what they thought was the truth

taboo

the things that are hardest to write:

- things we can't fathom, much like where energy goes after death or if we really die at all. much like, in a sense, what it feels like to survive after drowning, or how far away we are from finding life that isn't ours.
- the things we can't feel deeply enough—for instance, the rush of happiness after a win when we're feeling completely depressed after a loss, or the crashing feeling of grief when we're soaring inside.
- the tribute to the dear ones who we can only now hold dear in our hearts, for they have passed along to a place we've never been able to know yet. you can see it in the tears that splash on the page and smear the ink of your pen. once upon a time it was art, and now it's just tragedy.
- the burning ball of emotions swirling about your mind after someone tells you that you must censor them. oh, believe me, one of the hardest things to write is trying to tame a part of you that's finally been released from captivity, only to be told it can't go anywhere. the world is not about sheltering people from reality. the world needs class and the world needs reason, but the world does not need to be silenced.
- nothing. it's hard to write everything, but it's even harder to write nothing.

new things

a fresh start feels like
embracing reality enough to
forget the mistakes

a new day feels like
the sun streaming through
your windows, straight to your heart

another chance feels like
forgiveness may finally be
within reach

one more try feels like
breezing by without
the training wheels

and a clean slate feels like
the very first time
i looked into your eyes

growing up

fast-forward twenty years
to brownstone apartments
and the question,
"where has the time gone?"

too many memories escaped.
but they never left the place
where they will always remain,
in our ageless hearts

where pictures of us as smiling children are
still framed on my old dresser; where songs
from our youth still get stuck in my head
and where i can still hold you close

who cares about the miles between us
if i can still see you when i come home
for christmas; and our laughter feels like
i never left?

courage

find your heart from deep inside you
and embrace it;
paint a picture of what it sounds like
and write a song about its color
do not be afraid of who sees it
and do not push away those who
take the time to listen

something i want you to know (it's not impossible)

the world may pretend that people
fall into categories
or should be separated by societal norms

your gender, your color, your orientation
your religion, your money, your abilities and disabilities
should never suffice to define you

you are everything more than
simply what meets the eye; and
who you are is for you to decide

you must build everything
that you are made up of
don't let anyone else do it for you

the biggest mistake we make as people
is being so shallow that we forget
everyone is as equal as another

you are entitled to your opinion
but you are not entitled to demean someone else;
making them feel small won't make you any larger

we all deserve to receive our dreams.
we should not be denied our rights
or diminished by our character

if you've both worked hard,
you are just as deserving
as your opponent

don't give away something
or take it from another
just share it together

i'll hold your hand
if you hold mine because we're all just people
but together we are whole

let's keep joining hands with others until
no one is left out; everyone feels welcome
and the world is a dancing circle of love

epiphany

life is
simpler
than fiction

definitions

i believe everyone has a way to define themselves. a definition only we can uncover, a destiny only we can discover. our fate isn't left in anybody else's hands but our own.

this book is about describing what life means to me, and what it means to be on the way to finding the definition of yourself through your experiences. i'm still not done writing the meaning behind my name, because i believe it takes a lifetime, but we all explore and learn new things every day that contribute to who we are. everyone has a definition, but their definitions aren't always definite. they end in semicolons and always await a new way to be described. they use hyphens for names too long to spell by heart and ellipsis points when there's something else to be suspended by time.

our names are all words with definitions behind them. like words, we are each unique because we celebrate our own different meanings. we are all a new, completely different variation of simpler things, but we'll never be that simple, and we will never be the same. and like words, we'll never mean the same thing as another, but we have our own synonyms, and our own antonyms. we have prefixes and suffixes and origins, but we're never identical, we're just piled together beautifully enough to make words and music and sentences and metaphors. we can't write someone else's definition as much as they can't write ours. it wouldn't be my business to argue your meaning once you've already found it, just as it wouldn't be your business to contradict mine. we are all equally important in the great language of life, if there ever was something so elaborate.

we can be happy, sad, grieving, content, and everything in between; but no assumptions can be made just by looking at us. our definitions, while made up of words, are also about the way we express them; the way they are expressed by someone else. sometimes the emotion behind them is better kept to ourselves, but there comes a time when we must speak them aloud. no one can assume a conclusion or try to take power over something that's already ours: in the world of language, we all have something to say, but we're also willing to share our words, to exercise our right to reuse them; to use them to inspire someone else.

on a page, we appear as simple words clustered beside each other simply enough to create text. but we're more than that.

our definitions, our words, our names; even when they are strung together to convey a message, can be dissected, time after time after time, to reveal a new meaning.

our diversities are beautiful. we're made from different alphabets, garnished with different accents. we decide for ourselves who we want to be, what we want to say to the world.

we define who we are, but we still make people ponder what else we're made up of. we still make people create their own meanings for us and what we symbolize.

that's the beautiful thing about it all.

about the author

Kal Szarkowicz* is a writer and a poet. She plays the piano and the cello and loves music, literature, art, big cities, traveling and laughter. She lives in Minneapolis, Minnesota. This is her first book.

For more information about *definitions* or to order more copies of the book, visit petprojectpublishing.com.

*pronounced KAL SARR-koh-WITS